MY FIRST BOOK

PALESTINE

ALL ABOUT PALESTINE FOR KIDS

GL BED
CHILDREN BOOKS

Interior and cover Design: Daniel Day
Editor: Margaret Bam

For My Sons, Daniel, David and Jude

Friends Street, Ramallah, West Bank

Palestine

Palestine is a country.

A country is land that is controlled by a single government. Countries are also called nations, states, or nation-states.

Countries can be different sizes. Some countries are big and others are small.

Palestine

Where Is Palestine?

Palestine is located in the continent of Asia.

A continent is **a massive area of land that is separated from others** by water or other natural features.

Palestine is situated in the western part of Asia, specifically in the Middle East. Palestine shares borders with Israel to the east and the Mediterranean Sea to the west.

Yasser Arafat Grave, Ramallah

Capital

The city of Ramallah is the de facto capital of Palestine. However many Palestinians consider Jerusalem their rightful capital.

Ramallah and Jerusalem are both located in the region known as the West Bank. Ramallah is situated in the central part of the West Bank.

Gaza, also referred to as Gaza City, with a population of around 590,000 (in 2017), is the largest city in the State of Palestine.

Population

Palestine has population of around 5.4 million people making it the 121st most populated country in the world and the 37th most populated country in Asia.

In Palestine, the majority of the population lives in urban areas, particularly in cities and towns. Cities like Jerusalem, Ramallah, Nablus, Hebron, and Bethlehem have significant populations and serve as important economic, cultural, and administrative centers.

Gaza Strip, Palestine

Size

Palestine is **6,020 square kilometres** making it the 163rd largest country in the world.

Palestine is characterized by a range of landscapes, including coastal plains along the Mediterranean Sea, rolling hills and mountains in the central highlands, and the fertile Jordan Valley in the east.

Languages

The official language of Palestine is Arabic. Arabic is a beautiful language spoken by millions of people around the world, known for its rich history, poetic expressions, and lyrical sound. The Palestinian dialect of Arabic, known as Palestinian Arabic, is unique and carries its own distinct features and expressions.

Here are a few Arabic phrases

- شكرًا (Shukran) - Thank you Pronunciation: shoo-kran
- من فضلك (Min fadlak) - Please Pronunciation: min fad-lak

Golden dome of the rock in Jerusalem of Palestine.

Attractions

Palestine is home to many remarkable landmarks that showcase its rich history and cultural heritage.

Some beautiful places to visit in Palestine are

- **Dome of the Rock - An iconic golden-domed shrine in Jerusalem that holds religious significance for Muslims around the world.**
- **Church of the Nativity - Located in Bethlehem, believed to be the birthplace of Jesus Christ and a revered site for Christians.**

West Bank, Palestine

History of Palestine

People have lived in Palestine for thousands of years, with evidence of human settlement dating back to ancient times.

Throughout its history, Palestine has been a crossroads of civilizations, witnessing the rise and fall of empires, including the Canaanites, Israelites, Assyrians, Babylonians, Persians, Greeks, Romans, and many others.

Palestine's modern history includes the establishment of the State of Israel in 1948.

Bilin, Palestine

Customs in Palestine

Palestine is rich in customs and traditions that reflect its vibrant cultural heritage.

- One of the significant celebrations in Palestine is Eid al-Fitr, which marks the end of the holy month of Ramadan. Families come together to enjoy special meals, exchange gifts, and visit relatives and friends.
- Another important event is Palestinian weddings, which are joyous occasions filled with music, dancing, and traditional ceremonies.

Palestinian boy playing music

Music of Palestine

In Palestine, music plays an integral role in the cultural expression of its people.

One of the prominent musical forms is "Dabke," a lively and rhythmic dance music often accompanied by a line dance

Notable Palestinian musicians include Rim Banna, a renowned Palestinian singer known for her powerful voice and socially conscious lyrics, and Mohammed Assaf, a Palestinian singer who gained international recognition after winning the Arab Idol singing competition.

Mansaf

Food of Palestine

Palestine is renowned for its flavorful and diverse cuisine, which reflects the region's rich culinary heritage and cultural influences.

Mansaf is a traditional Palestinian dish that holds great significance and is often considered to be the national dish of the country. It features tender lamb or chicken cooked in a tangy yogurt sauce and served over a bed of fragrant rice or bulgur. It is often garnished with toasted almonds and pine nuts, adding a delightful crunch.

Food of Palestine

Palestinian cuisine embraces the use of aromatic spices, fresh herbs, olive oil, and locally sourced ingredients. Popular dishes include

- **Makloubeh - A one-pot meal featuring layers of rice, vegetables (such as eggplant, cauliflower, and carrots), and meat (like chicken or lamb).**
- **Musakhan - A traditional Palestinian dish that showcases the flavors of sumac-spiced roasted chicken served on top of a bed of caramelized onions and flatbread.**
- **Falafel - A popular dish made from ground chickpeas.**

Milk Grotto Church, Bethlehem, Palestine

Weather in Palestine

Palestine experiences a Mediterranean climate, characterized by hot and dry summers, and mild and rainy winters.

Summers in Palestine, particularly during July and August, are typically hot with temperatures often exceeding 30°c. Winters in Palestine are relatively mild, with temperatures ranging from around 8°c to 15°c. Spring and autumn offer pleasant temperatures, making them popular seasons for outdoor activities and exploring the natural beauty of Palestine.

Stripped hyena

Animals of Palestine

Palestine is home to a diverse range of fascinating animals. Some of the notable animals found in Palestine include:

1. **Palestine Mountain Gazelle: A graceful and endangered species, known locally as "Ibex," with its distinct curved horns and agile movements.**
2. **Striped Hyena: A nocturnal animal with a unique striped coat, known for its scavenging habits and ability to adapt to various habitats.**

Jordan River

Rivers

Palestine is home to several rivers, here are some notable rivers in Palestine:

1. Jordan River: The Jordan River forms the eastern border of Palestine and separates it from Jordan.
2. Yarkon River: The Yarkon River is a river in central Israel that flows through parts of Palestine, including the West Bank.
- Nahal Sorek: Nahal Sorek is a seasonal river that flows through parts of the West Bank and Israel.

Sports of Palestine

Sports also hold significant importance in Palestinian culture.

Here are some notable sportspeople from Palestine:

1. **Mahmoud Sarsak - Football:** Mahmoud Sarsak is a former Palestinian football player who represented the national team.
2. **Nader Al-Masri - Athletics:** Nader Al-Masri is a Palestinian long-distance runner.
3. **Abdel Nasser Barakat - Football:** Abdel Nasser Barakat is a Palestinian football coach and former player.

Leila Khaled

Famous

Palestine is home to numerous talented people. Here are some notable figures from Palestine:

- **Edward Said - Intellectual and Author:** Edward Said was a prominent Palestinian-American intellectual, literary critic, and author.
- **Mahmoud Darwish - Poet:** Mahmoud Darwish was a celebrated Palestinian poet and writer.
- **Leila Khaled - Activist:** Leila Khaled is a Palestinian political activist known for her involvement in the Palestinian resistance movement.

Gaza Strip, Palestine

Something Extra...

As an additional treat, here are some lesser-known facts about Palestine:

1. Palestine is home to one of the oldest olive trees in the world, known as the "Tree of Life." This ancient olive tree, estimated to be over 5,000 years old.
2. The city of Hebron, located in the West Bank, is home to the Ibrahimi Mosque, also known as the Cave of the Patriarchs. A significant religious site for both Muslims and Jews.
3. The Palestinian keffiyeh is a traditional headscarf worn by many Palestinians.

Hebron, Palestine

Words From the Author

We hope that you enjoyed learning about the wonderful country of Palestine.

Palestine is a country rich in culture and beauty, with lots of wonderful places to visit and people to meet.

We hope you continue to learn more about this wonderful nation. If you enjoyed this book, consider leaving a review!

With Love

Printed in Great Britain
by Amazon

29768611R00025